It's Not Just a Game

It's Not Just a Game

My Journey From the Streets to Professional Basketball

Eric Crookshank

Nimbus
Publishing

Copyright © 2012, Eric Crookshank

All rights reserved. No part of this book may be reproduced, stored in a retrieval system or transmitted in any form or by any means without the prior written permission from the publisher, or, in the case of photocopying or other reprographic copying, permission from Access Copyright, 1 Yonge Street, Suite 1900, Toronto, Ontario M5E 1E5.

Nimbus Publishing Limited
3731 Mackintosh St, Halifax, NS B3K 5A5
(902) 455-4286 nimbus.ca

Printed and bound in Canada

Design: Jenn Embree

Library and Archives Canada Cataloguing in Publication

Crookshank, Eric
It's not just a game : my journey from the streets to professional basketball / Eric Crookshank.
ISBN 978-1-55109-959-0

1. Crookshank, Eric. 2. Basketball players—Nova Scotia—Biography. 3. Halifax Rainmen (Basketball team). I. Title.

GV884.C76A3 2012   796.323092   C2012-905810-6

Nimbus Publishing acknowledges the financial support for its publishing activities from the Government of Canada through the Canada Book Fund (CBF) and the Canada Council for the Arts, and from the Province of Nova Scotia through the Department of Communities, Culture and Heritage.

Contents

	Prologue	vii
Chapter 1	In the Beginning	1
Chapter 2	Learning Lessons	27
Chapter 3	The Road to the Rainmen	45
Chapter 4	"Air Canada" Takes Off	75
Chapter 5	Giving Back	93
	Epilogue	109
	About the Author	112

PROLOGUE

Standing in St. Patrick's-Alexandra School with 160 eyes fixated on me, with children waiting to hear the next words out of my mouth, I think to myself: *When I was that age, I was watching people's lives stolen by gunshots and drugs in the 69th Village of Oakland, California, and here they are looking to me as inspiration. Who am I today to motivate this type of admiration?*

I thought back to the days when I walked my younger sister, Shirley, through alleyways reeking of filth—past drug dealers working for their livelihood—and tried to shield her from this world and guide her as a parent would. I thought of my mother, who may have been trapped in those same alleyways, lost in the same dealings I worked so hard to keep Shirley from—even that hadn't slowed my determination to protect my baby sister. I walked on a road of self-guidance, shielded only by my faith. The only dream in my fifteen-year-old mind had been to survive.

I have enjoyed a successful career as a basketball player, most recently with the Halifax Rainmen NBL team, and I am a happy husband and father. Where I am today all started from the bottom. I want to tell the story of my journey from there to here. Today I live my life led by faith, but that wasn't always the case. Growing up, I had obstacles to overcome: gangs, drugs, poverty, and murder are just the beginning.

Chapter 1
In the Beginning

From the first days of my life I had big shoes to fill. I was born November 13, 1978, at Alta Bates Hospital in Berkeley, California. My father was a 6'6", 240-pound basketball legend, and a fierce street gangster—captain on the court as well as in the streets. Growing up, I was unaware of his wrongs; he led by example and I followed willingly.

My father played basketball for Lake Marriott University in Oakland. He worked the court like he worked the streets: with vengeance, confidence, and total control. I looked up to him like he was the president. His passions, basketball and life on the streets, were instilled in me from a young age. I always had a ball in my hand, but my skills would not advance until much later in life. Drumming was my real talent then, and is still very much my passion. (I learned from watching the drummer at our church. I picked up my first drumsticks at age five, and fell in love with music.)

My mother was full of sunshine. She had a glowing personality and a fantastic sense of humour. Everything she did was for her family. Even when my father began to climb his way up the hierarchy of the streets, she climbed by his side. Their relationship was one of genuine companionship.

When my father graduated from university, our family moved to Galveston, Texas. I remember my father being extremely loving at that time. I felt totally surrounded by love and support. My mother, father, older brother Terrill, younger sister Shirley, and me, were extremely close, and the bond with our extended family became a significant part of my upbringing.

King of the Streets

The street side of my father wasn't nearly as clean. He was the king, and Cedar Terrance Projects in Galveston was his court. He had his hands deep in the drug game, and basketball soon became irrelevant. With every street corner under his reign, money flowed freely and respect was given absolutely. Respect in the game equals power, and my father's power was far-reaching. His name alone instilled fear in those who were allowed in his company. His Ford truck would pull up, and my father, with his chiselled frame, would be sitting on his favourite lawn chair in the back. He was always the passenger, never the driver, making himself clearly visible to the world. No shirt, shining jewelry, and shoes without laces: this was my father's uniform. Two taps on the roof of the truck was his sign to stop. Then he would skip off the back to speak to anyone who called his name. I spent weeks out of school, taking my father around the blocks so he could check on his territory. But he was always generous to a fault with his family. If I asked for money to make a candy run to the store, my father would peel a hundred-dollar bill off the knot he carried in his pocket at all times. Trying to return his change would result only in a kiss and a soft "boy, please."

I can remember driving my father's truck into the projects one day when I was ten years old. At this young age I was already playing chauffeur to the kingpin. He hopped out of the back, sparks flying from the two shotguns he had hidden under his trench coat. I can still hear the "whip" of the coat when he hauled the shotguns from their hiding place, the explosions, firing one after the other from each hand, aimed as a warning to the petty dealer who had made the mistake of owing my father money. Shots rang out through windows and into the air past people standing in the afternoon sun. Fear ran down my face, urine down my legs. My body trembled as my father jumped back on the bed of the truck, yelling at me to drive away. Not three hours later, money was paid to him. The compassionate part of my father returned to those same projects later that day with money in hand, offering to pay for any damages his earlier rampage had caused.

These memories are still vivid. With my seven-year-old cousin, Shakieta, at my side, I would be up until all hours of the early morning counting thousands of dollars of drug money. Sleep was never a promise in my father's house. When there was money to be counted we would be hauled from our beds by a drunken father, shaken awake, and sat in front of a pile of bills. Bags of cash would be shoved in our faces. If the count was off by a single dollar, there would be trouble.

One particularly significant memory is of being held to the end of my father's pistol the one night my counting skills were off. I had counted twenty thousand dollars and recorded two thousand dollars by mistake, which sent my father into a drunken rage. Alcohol thick in his veins, he cocked his gun and pushed it to my temple, threatening that the next time his money was counted wrong, it would be the last. The taste of death soaked my throat. I thought I was going to die. Fortunately, his coordination was off due to his intoxication level. He pulled the gun away from my head and exaggerated his threat with wild gestures. The deafening crack of the gun going off brought absolute terror to my soul. My father had managed to shoot himself in the finger, not even realizing it for several minutes as he struggled to regain his composure. I was overwhelmed over those few minutes with the realization that I was still alive. I had been sure I was dead.

Even with so many years devoted to the drug game, my father was arrested only once. Settled in the back seat of his silver and maroon Cadillac with a bag of cocaine in the trunk, cold beer by his feet, and his brother driving, he was surrounded by police, guns drawn, yelling at him to get out. Hands on the car and shirtless as usual, my father was thrown into a police car and brought to jail. Police officers began their effort to intimidate him, threatening to charge him with possession. "Possession of what?" was his only response. Being well trained in his trade, he began schooling the officers on how fingerprints could never be lifted off the duct-taped package that had just happened to be in the car at the time of his arrest.

My father told this story with enthusiasm, remembering how, as he put it, "the police huddled, heads together, like a football team calling their next play." They told him he would be up for a fifty-thousand-dollar bail. My father refused. He said if any money was to be paid it would be reimbursement to him for the cold beer ruined in the back seat of his car while he awaited his release. Beer was a staple in my father's life. Surrounded by hardcore drugs, dealers, and users, my father relied heavily on alcohol, but never the drugs that had bought him the life he had become accustomed to. With evidence to convict my father lacking, he was released that day. Although prepared for the day when arrest might become a reality, my father would wake me with four hundred dollars every morning, just in case that was the day bail would be required.

The Price

Through everything, my father cherished me as though I was his most valuable possession. I was treated like the heir to his throne, and life in Texas was privileged under my father's reign. I was always the best dressed and was highly respected, solely on the basis of who my father was. But material belongings were the centres of our lives. Money was easy, and work was pointless while my father ruled. My mother, while helping my father package his drugs, became addicted.

I watched my mother deteriorate physically, mentally, and spiritually. I was eleven years old when she dropped—at least to my young eyes—about fifty pounds in a matter of months. My father was immersed so deeply in his own world that he didn't seem to notice the change. But watching my mother kept me from ever touching the drugs myself. When my maternal grandmother took notice of the effects this lifestyle was having on my mother and our whole family, she took us with her when she accepted a job offer in California. My grandmother kept my mother's addiction hidden from my father so that he wouldn't stop us from leaving with her when she so desperately needed our love and support. My mother was given the opportunity to move to California and get clean, or stay in Texas and allow her addiction to consume her entirely. Little did we know, but the true grime would begin when we moved into the 69th Village in Oakland, California.

69TH VILLAGE PROJECTS

I was twelve years old when my grandmother, Shirley Crookshank, became my guiding light. Along with my mother and I, she took my nine-year-old sister and fifteen-year-old brother to California with her. She wanted to rescue us from the circumstances in Texas. Although we left behind what seemed like a life of royalty only to enter into one with very little material substance, my love for my sister and my faith would keep me going. Thinking that our living situation would improve, I had been excited to move to California. We lived with our grandmother for a short time, and then with my aunt. But with my mother still addicted and my aunt trying to get her to change her ways, my mother knew she would need to move out in order to live the way she saw best for herself. This is when I was introduced to the 69th Village Projects. The 69th Village had a high school with an average of three murders every year, and was located in the middle of a heavy drug-dealing neighbourhood. I remember leaving school one day and seeing the body of a young boy who had been shot and left on campus.

The first time we drove into the projects I thought my grandmother must have wanted us to drown in despair. With thirteen-year-old eyes, I looked around and saw drug slinging on every corner. These were dirty dealers, unafraid of death. The alleyways between the housing complexes were full of filth and garbage. The unforeseen circumstances of life in the California projects quickly became evident. My mother's addiction only got worse. In her pursuit of a high she would leave us alone for months at a time. Slowly losing my mother to addiction ate away at my soul. I had to become a guardian for my little sister, Shirley, at a time in my life when I could barely take care of myself. Our older brother had gone to live with our grandfather. Terrill had long been considered the favourite, and when given the opportunity to escape, he went willingly. But my sister and I refused to leave our mother's side.

My father abandoned us after we left with our mother. Financial assistance from him was cut off, leaving us with no support. This was hard for me to understand. In Texas my mother had kept her addiction hidden, as my father would have been furious. But without him to lose, she embraced the life of a drug addict. With my older brother now living with our grandfather in Vallejo, California, I became the man of the house. My mother's addiction became my secret. I refused to tell my family the extent of it, afraid that they would take us away from her. My love for my mother was unconditional, and my loyalty undying.

Gang affiliation is what kept people alive in the 69th Village. There, you were a part of the gang or you were nobody. In the first month of moving to Oakland I was "jumped in." Seven grown men beat me so badly I missed school for a week. There was no money for doctors, so my limbs ached for months—a constant reminder of the world I knew I would have to adapt to. The hood became my family. They would protect my sister and me when my mother couldn't. I kept this from Shirley, as I never wanted to inspire her to become part of what I had had no choice but to embrace. It is not a life I would want for any other child.

In order to keep the lights on, I got a job as lookout for the dealers on the block. My job was to whistle a warning at the sign of any police. After school I would pick Shirley up and walk her home to make sure she stayed safe. I would settle her in our apartment for the evening, make sure she was fed and had done her homework. When she was safe in bed, I would head back out to start my night shift on the corner. On Sundays I would play drums at our local church. I was given donations in exchange for entertaining the congregation—they knew that Shirley and I needed the help.

The situation in the village became critical the day a man broke into our home. He was after the guns my mother kept hidden for the dealers who lived around us—a hiding place paid for by cocaine. The man walked past my bedroom in the dark of night. Seeing only his shadow heading toward my mother's bedroom, I was terrified. He turned to go to the kitchen. My mother heard the noise and got up to see what it was. I was quaking in my bed, only thirteen years old, knowing I should warn her but scared silent. When I heard my mother scream, I rushed to her side. The man had hit her on the head with a wrench. She was lying on the kitchen floor unconscious and in a pool of blood. I ran out of the house after him. I ran in my underwear, with nothing to protect me. I ran blinded by fury and in an effort to protect everything I loved. The realization that my mother was close to death came only when I ran back to the apartment to a scene of blood, and the tears and screams of my ten-year-old sister.

Temporary Recovery

My mother was in the hospital for weeks. We stayed with our aunt, praying for her recovery. When my mother was better we moved back to 69th Village. We had hopes that this incident would end her affair with drugs, but even a near-death experience couldn't keep her away.

It was only a month after my mother came home from the hospital that she left us again. My sister and I were alone in our apartment. I would cry myself to sleep every night with the constant fear of my mother's attacker returning. I felt totally abandoned. With our phone now cut off, I also felt shut out from the world. I had to walk to a pay phone to speak to anyone beyond my neighbourhood.

When my mother was home she was very caring. She would spend time praying with us, instilling our faith. To this day, religion is a huge part of who I am.

My faith has taken me through the most difficult times in my life, and has led me to where I stand now. But after a few months of quality time spent with her family, my mother would be gone again, her battle with addiction calling her back into the streets.

She continued this pattern of coming home, spending time with us for awhile, and then leaving again. She'd tell us she would be back, but we never knew when. My sister and I would watch hours pass and weeks wander by with no sign of her. We were left wondering whether or not our mother's love was genuine. She taught us about faith and prayer, but subjected us to abandonment and doubt. Hesitation gave way to distrust in my faith. I began questioning my beliefs.

My mother had no secondary education and never had a real job when we were young. We relied on food stamps and were provided with housing by Section 8 (social assistance). I had gone from having everything I desired and the confidence that came with that, to having to fight for every dollar and become a parent to my little sister. I would make sure Shirley ate her dinner: Top Ramen noodles with hot dogs or Top Ramen noodles with cheese or eggs—whatever we could find or borrow from a neighbour. The fifty dollars I would get each day from working lookout for would go to pay for food. Our staples were bread, milk, cereal, Kool-Aid, and, of course, Top Ramen noodles. On cold nights we had to turn the oven on and leave the door open to keep warm: this became our only source of heat when the lights got turned off. My mother was often unable to or forgot to pay the bills. We never knew which.

My father's home and the security of his money seemed so far away. I dreamed of leaving this place behind. My sister and I had developed a bond through our years fending for ourselves, but I knew that if I shared our secret we would be taken away from our mother. I was scared that if my father found out the truth, he would send for us and my mother would be left to her own means. I was not going to leave her. I knew she could not survive without us.

Making a Move

After all the negative things we went through in Oakland, my mother finally made the decision to get clean and move our family to a better school district in Vallejo, where my brother had been living with my grandfather. In Vallejo, my sister and I could get a better education in a safer school.

My sister, mother, and I moved to Vallejo with my grandmother that summer. There, we were reunited with the mother we had known and loved before drugs had stolen her from us. But I was still fighting with my emotions at this point: I wasn't sure if I loved or hated my mother. After putting my sister and me through so much, hearing lie after lie from her, and having had so many promises broken, I was still unsure if I could trust her to stay clean. I waited for my mother to prove herself to us. I wanted to make sure my sister and I would be okay.

My Mother's Light

My mother continued on her road to recovery and proved herself to us. She established herself in her own home and began to lead a clean life. She was the charismatic mother I had defended for all those years, the mother who taught me the value of respect, how to live spiritually, and how to be grateful. My mother was my inspiration; she was what I lived for. She was charming, outgoing, and lively. She was fearless, bold, and blunt, and a force to be reckoned with. She was an avid churchgoer, devoted to her faith, and embraced the congregation as her other family. She is the reason that I still pray and believe so strongly in my faith, even though I once had my doubts.

After we were settled in our new home, my brother, Terrill, moved back in with us. I was thrilled to have my big brother back, but part of me resented him for having left us in the projects only to come back to us now, when we were on a better path. To this day he feels a sting of guilt when we talk about this time in our life, but I know that it wasn't his choice or his fault.

Living in Vallejo, I had to leave behind the constant shield I had carried through my years in the projects and attempt to embrace the calmer and kinder atmosphere of my new home. Not walking on the lawn of the school was one of the most critical issues we had to deal with here. I had grown accustomed to worrying about gunshots and drug dealers. This was a different world for me.

I also went from being a great student in Oakland to being one of the worst in Vallejo. The best students in Oakland could not touch the higher standards of the Vallejo public school system. I still had a street mentality, which caused nothing but conflict in my classes. Suspensions were frequent. Disrespecting the teachers, skipping classes, and clowning around were a few of the reasons I would be sent home on a regular basis. My grandmother would joke that she was going to put a desk in the garage because I was home so often. Transitioning from the life I knew to what was expected of me was difficult.

My attitude changed dramatically when I met my new best friends: Henry, CC, Carlton, Tyson, Jaccarri, Tony, and Brandon. You could say they saved my life. We shared the struggles of single-parent homes, and pasts riddled with drug addiction, gangs, and violence. We motivated each other to do better, and together we navigated our way through high school. With most of our fathers out of the picture, we became each other's examples of how to be men. This bond has continued to evolve throughout our lives, and we still rely heavily on each other for advice, support, and guidance.

LEARNING THE GAME

Being in high school with my new friends, I found myself more at peace with my mother. And because I finally felt safe, and no longer had to take care of my sister and look out for my mother, I was able to focus on myself. This was when I first began to devote my time to improving my basketball skills. I wanted to play basketball in Vallejo because each game was an event: bands, cheerleaders, and fans embraced basketball culture. In Oakland, games had been played right after school in order to avoid any evening shootouts.

When I moved to Vallejo, I had not yet developed my basketball skills, because I hadn't had any time to practice while living in the projects. At my new home, I began to practice with Brandon Armstrong, CC Sabathia, Tyson Davis, and Henry Frasier. Every time we played together I would get beaten badly. This drove me to be better.

I tried out for the basketball team in grade ten and made it, but I sat on the bench the whole year. I practiced hard, had heart and potential, but no real skills. In eleventh grade I didn't make the team. My spirits were shattered when I saw that my friends had all made it, and I was the only one who wouldn't be playing that year. My desire to be a part of that world drove me to embrace my other passion in life: drumming. Although I never learned how to read music, I was the best drummer in my high school. I had made the conscious decision to stay away from learning how to read music, as I felt like it would handicap me. I wanted music to come from my soul, so I felt the music, playing by ear. Because I couldn't play basketball I joined the marching band, and played snare drum on the sidelines that whole year.

Drumming Up Trouble

During that year off from basketball I had a lot more time on my hands, so I went on a mission to occupy myself. I saw a poster advertising drumming auditions for a big-time gospel singer who was coming to town. I auditioned and was selected. For two years on weekends, evenings, and in the summer I played with this gospel artist during his western tour dates. I enjoyed it, but after awhile I began to journey down the wrong road. Finding myself becoming more and more popular in town and on tour, I began to let my ego take over and started to embrace the nightlife in the cities we played in, even though I was still underage. One night, after staying up late partying, I returned to the hotel with a friend and happened upon the singer in the lobby. Being a religious person, he was extremely disappointed in my behaviour, and I was let go from the tour. He was trying to promote a healthy lifestyle, while I was more focused on myself. My over-confidence had tricked me into thinking that no matter how I behaved, my talents would keep me in the limelight.

I had been underage when I signed my contract with the tour, so my mother had been required to give her permission. This meant that she was contacted when I was let go from the tour. I could see disappointment written all over my mother's face when I got home. She had been so proud of my successes and here I was letting her down.

Earning My Spot

During my third and final year of high school, I did it all. I played in the marching band throughout the football season. I made the basketball team that year as well, and played the few months after band finished. It wasn't until later that I found out the basketball coach thought I was a leech. My best friends all had serious promise in professional sports or educational opportunities: CC was headed to the MLB, Brandon to the NBA, Henry to the NFL, and Carlton, the genius, had already been recruited by several Ivy League schools. The coach that year made me sell candy as a fundraiser to secure my place on the team. During that year, being a six-foot, two-inch point guard, I was known for my shooting and ball-handling skills. I dominated on the court when I was given the chance, but only played two games that year.

Still, my mother supported everything I did. Every single event my friends and I were a part of, she was there, vocal and proud. She went from hands-off to hands entirely on. I can remember her being decked out, head to toe, in my name. She would take T-shirts and decorate them with markers, with my name in big, bright letters. Her jeans would have my name etched down the front, displaying her pride. She would yell and scream, making sure everyone knew she was there—she definitely made sure I knew she was there! It was embarrassing, but nothing made me happier. I embraced my mother's enthusiasm. I played my absolute hardest to show her how proud she should be.

Chapter 2
Learning Lessons

When I graduated high school, I had mixed emotions: should I be happy, or should I be sad that I was graduating and had no real goals? I came full circle: I graduated and went back to my father. I flew back to Texas to work for my now-legitimate father. Everything had changed when he had stopped drinking. He had started a landscaping company during my years away, and when I returned he had me managing his business. Business was real, life was great, and materialism had taken a back seat to his family. Working hard every day, I would come home exhausted, but I was saving money. I can remember yelling at my stepmom for washing my clothes wrong, since everything was getting too small for me to wear. I couldn't understand why nothing would fit.

My father had me working so hard that it left me little time to have any fun. I got frustrated one day and decided I would quit. When I told my father I was done, he told me that once you graduated you had to be a man, and men work. He passed me a Burger King uniform and told me to go work for my cousin, who managed a local franchise at the time. I lasted all of a week and went right back to my father. I jumped back on my lawn mower and continued to landscape. But this time every lawn I left behind had my initials on the side, carved with a weed whacker.

Henry

I had been reading in the newspapers about all my friends doing incredible things when the phone calls started to come in. Tyson was trying to manage a popular band at the time, but he was forgetting to do small things—leaving luggage behind, for example—and his position was shaky. Brandon was struggling with his eligibility for the following year and had decided to enter the NBA draft, leaving his schooling behind. Carlton, who was used to having perfect grades, saw his marks falling. CC was phoning me, stressed out about his contract in major league baseball. It seemed like all of us were falling apart at the same time. Then I got the call from my mother that Henry had been beat up by some guys at his school and was in the hospital with his jaw wired shut. I ran to my father, told him what had happened, and he put me on a flight home. I walked off the flight in California, and everyone I had known for years was shocked when they saw me. After being in Texas for eight months, I returned at six-feet, eight inches tall. Now I understood why my clothes had been shrinking!

I went to the hospital to check on Henry and tried my best to convince him to tell me who had jumped him so that I could take care of them. He wouldn't give me any information about it, so I made my decision: I would go back to school with Henry to make sure he always stayed safe. I applied to Chabot Junior College, which Henry had been attending, before returning to Texas for the summer to finish working with my father.

I was thrilled when I got the phone call telling me I had been accepted. It seemed like forces beyond my control had been looking out for me. Before I had learned of Henry's fight at school I had been speaking with my cousin, who was still involved in my father's previous business endeavours. I had asked if he could get me involved as well. I had seen my father making more money than he would ever need when I was young, and I was tempted to follow his path. With hesitation, my cousin had agreed and had a package on the way for me when I left for California. The decision to return to school with Henry and the blessing of being accepted were events that could not have come at a better time. My life could have taken a very different road, and I believe that I have my prayers to thank for delivering a better and straighter path to my doorstep.

Chabot Junior College

September came, and the basketball court at Chabot Junior College was mine. I hadn't practiced at all while I had been in Texas, so when I got back in the gym I was shocked that all of a sudden I could dunk. The coach saw that I had some real talent. I had finally found my rhythm, and the team dominated. Attendance when I played went from 800 people per game to 2,500. I remember seeing Bobby Knight, the famous Indiana University coach, scouting on the sidelines. Knowing he was there made me play my absolute hardest. I wanted to show him I was capable of playing at a high level. He asked to speak to me after the game. This excited me, as Henry would be attending Indiana University the following year and had told me I was on their recruitment radar. I was soon getting up to ten handwritten letters a week from universities everywhere: Kansas State, Missouri, Arizona, and Oregon, to name a few. There were stacks of letters everywhere. My mother's pride radiated from head to toe.

I laughed when I saw her using some of the letters as coasters. "We aren't going there anyway," she would say. We were a never-ending team, my mother and I.

Coaches from all types of schools had been coming to watch my games at Chabot. I signed with Idaho State University that year and planned to start my first season in a new school with a bang. I had talent, but my grades were still poor, and I was let go from Idaho State.

I was given another chance at USC Los Angeles thanks to coach Henry Bibby helping me with my application. I had everything and more provided for me there, a full scholarship, room and board, books, and a living allowance. I was living better every day. But I wasn't allowed any time on the court since I couldn't keep my grades where they needed to be. I decided to transfer schools again, this time to California State, Dominguez Hills.

Dominguez Hills, 2001–2004

Dominguez Hills was a smaller school with a smaller basketball program, but it was there that I learned I had to stop half-stepping through life. I worked hard to keep my grades up. I took business and music, and succeeded on the court for three years as a Dominguez Hills Toro. We played in the NCAA Division II under coach Damaine Powell, and what I remember most about my experience on the team is the size and sound of the crowds at the games. The spirit of our fellow students would always energize us and push us harder to win. I had a real opportunity to connect with my teammates, as the same players stayed with the team for their university career. We had time to develop a real dynamic. I was elected team captain all three years and led the league in rebounds.

The teachers at Dominguez Hills changed my outlook on school work. They were down to earth and had lived the same type of life I had. Falling in love with their style made me fall in love with my program. I started to set goals for my life and thought about my future after graduation. All I wanted to do was play basketball. Every spare moment I had was spent in the gym working on my game. I decided I would take my team to the championship, and would do whatever it took to get us there. Night in, night out, I was focused on basketball, as much as my mother had been focused on her addiction. It would seem I had learned some good things from my mother's time on the streets.

Despite my successes, I soon began to get homesick. I would fly home almost every weekend I wasn't playing just so I could be close to my family. Every time I was home, I would take the opportunity to go back to my church and spend the morning with my other passion: drums. I finally began to appreciate what I had been given. So many of the students at Dominguez Hills were working to pay their way through school, and everything I had was taken care of. After applying myself in all areas of my life, my grades rose and everything seemed to get better. I knew at this point that I had talent as a basketball player, but that it would be up to me to make Eric Crookshank who he needed to be as a man. The silver platter was on the table, ready for me to eat. There were times when I couldn't find a spoon, but I pushed on.

My major, math, became my love. From my first lessons in math, sitting in my father's house counting drug dollars, to a business degree, it seemed almost unreal that this was the path that had been set before me. I graduated as a first-team All-American from California State, Dominguez Hills. I brought my degree—business administration with a minor in music—home, full of pride, knowing I was the first person in my immediate family to graduate from college.

Darkest Days

Only weeks after graduating university, my mother, who had not been feeling quite herself, went for testing at Kaiser Permanente Vallejo Medical Center, a hospital that caters to people on social assistance. Many of the doctors were just out of school. They told my mother that she had cancer in her ovaries, but that they would perform a hysterectomy to remove them, and she would be okay. My mother had just begun to find her way in life, running her own childcare business, and living clean. But in California, and the United States in general, health care is very expensive. Most Americans will have medical coverage provided by their jobs, but because my mother owned her own business, she had none. We knew it might be difficult to find the money to cover these expenses. It turned out that she would receive some support from Medi-Cal insurance, and she had saved a bit of money. It would be enough to get the surgery.

The surgery was booked within days and my mother was admitted to the hospital. The surgery seemed to go well, and life became happy again. We thought this meant she would be healthy, so we threw parties at home—partially to take our mind off any negative thoughts, partially to celebrate my mother's life. When my mother returned from the hospital, my sister and I were there to take care of her. At this point I was living at home since I had just graduated and was still trying to figure out what I wanted to do with my life. I helped my mother with her childcare business.

My mother would always tell us things would be okay, so when she came home, my friends, family, and I were all relieved that she was going to be fine and that our lives could continue as they had before. But a few weeks after returning home, my mother and I were sitting on the porch when she started to feel pains in her stomach where she had had her surgery. Over the next few days, she stopped eating and sleeping and was in constant pain. We knew something was very wrong. She went back to the doctor. They ran tests, poked and prodded her, and three days later we received a phone call asking us to come in to discuss the results. The doctors told us that, during the surgery, they had missed some sections that had been affected by the cancer. This meant that the cancer had spread throughout her abdomen. They compared her body to a beehive that had been poked with a stick: as soon as you poke the hive, the bees come swarming out. This was the effect the cancer now had inside my mother.

Nine days after my mother began to feel pains in her stomach, she had lost almost sixty pounds after having gone through chemo treatment, and had faded, physically, to only a portion of what she had been. I can remember going to visit my mother in her hospital room and she was laughing. I asked why she was laughing, and she said she was happy with her life. She started to tell me that she was proud of her children. We knew she was thinking about death and that she had accepted it. She wanted us not to worry, but all we could think of was how desolate life would be without her in it. Even at this time in her life she felt she needed to take care of us, when it was she who needed the care.

My mother asked for my family members, my friends, and I to each come in, individually, to speak with her. She told CC that he needed to follow whatever path made him happiest, whether that was professional baseball or not, reminding him that money wasn't the only thing that made him happy. She told Henry and Carlton never to give up on anything. She told Terrill that she knew he would follow the word of God. She told my sister to stay true to herself and live a happy life. She told me that I needed to do what I was put on earth to do: play basketball, play drums, and take care of my sister. She also told me I needed to make my relationship with my father as strong as it could be.

She told us there was to be no crying and that we needed to make the best of our lives, to never settle for anything less than what we capable of. She told us to be good parents when we had children: to love them like she loved us, to treat our daughters like princesses and our sons like kings, as she had. She told us that if she could beat addiction and live a happy life, we could do anything, and to never let the little things bother us. The doctors had told my mother that she had three days left, but she kept this to herself, as she didn't want us to worry.

After I spent three full days in the hospital at her side, she told me to go home and get some rest. I woke up the next morning to phone calls telling me to come to the hospital to spend time with the family. I walked into the hospital and there were about forty people waiting for me. When I got into my mother's room I could see her, with her head bald from her chemo treatments and the tumour now pushing out of her stomach. She looked like she was pregnant and her stomach was hard to the touch. Overnight, her body had given up and she had been put on a machine to help her breathe. The tumour had been too much for her small body and had pushed on her lungs. They took my mother off life-support once I arrived.

Grief

At this point I went to a very dark place. I lost my faith. I went through a whole month and a half where I couldn't leave my house, could barely eat, could not function at all. When I tried to sleep, I had nightmares. I had a hard time dealing with my relationship with my father because I felt like he should have given my mother more support. My friends were on edge around me, never knowing how I might react to anything they said. I tried my best to think of the positive, to stay on the track my mother would have wanted, but I became unable to. The positive thoughts did nothing to lift the sadness and grief that weighed on my heart and my soul. I felt I had nothing left to do but turn to the negative. I hurt uncontrollably. My mother's love was gone. I would never see or hear her in the physical form again. I didn't know what to do. Basketball didn't exist to me. I couldn't think about the rest of my life. I couldn't imagine living my life without my mother.

Eventually I realized I had to come back. I leaned on my ever-present friends and listened to my brother's inspiration. Terrill would pass me index cards every day with scriptures that he felt strongly about and thought might guide me. Scriptures fed my soul every time I read them. I found safety in reading my own Bible and saw that the situations described were comparable to this life and the people in these stories learned to live again. This promise inspired me to begin to live my own life again. My mother had told me I would be okay, so this is what I would strive for. I felt the need to let everyone know that

I was Yvonne Crookshank's son. I wanted to make my mother's name shine. I wanted people to be impressed that my mother had raised good children and for her to be proud in her afterlife. I would find myself driving and crying, regretting any times I may have disrespected her. I learned the scripture "honour thy mother and father" and I vowed then to never disrespect my mother or her memory. I had the mindset that everything happens for a reason. I lost my mother and was led back to my roots and my faith.

My sister Shirley also closed herself to the world for many months. For a long time she was unable to control her emotions, and when a thought crossed her mind, no matter where she was, she would become hysterical. Her friends were the only ones who could pull her out of this. Shirley had been our mother's princess, and she did not know how to live without her.

Terrill, to this day, has problems with the loss of our mother. He is now a minister and has followed the word of God, as she said he would. He speaks about lessons he learned through this experience frequently. He speaks about forgiveness and making amends, appreciating what and who you have while you have them. Losing a parent brings siblings together in an unexplainable way. We had to lean on each other. My friends had a hard time as well: my mother had also been a mother to them, and they had loved her in an incredible way.

Months after my mother passed away, I would take her ashes with me wherever I went. I can remember calling friends and telling them, "Mom and I are coming to visit." They never questioned me and were happy to feel her presence again. We would even play dominos with my mother watching over us from her urn on the table. Today my mother's memory is with me always. I thought about her while I played at the Halifax Metro Centre with the Rainmen. If only my mother were there it would sound like ten thousand fans. Her death was the worst thing to happen to me in my life, but I found the positive way out. I knew that if I could live through that, I could live through anything.

Knowing that April 8, 2003, the most difficult day of my life, has come and gone, I share my mother's legacy with you now. The positive aspects of my mother far outweigh any negative times we had. She is my daily inspiration. To this day her spirit lives through my words, and I hear myself saying things to my own daughter that she would have said to me and my brother and sister. Life truly is a rollercoaster, but no matter how deep down it goes, if you have your seat belt of faith on tightly, you'll always come back up to see sunlight in the end.

Chapter 3
The Road to the Rainmen

The summer after I lost my mother I returned to Los Angeles instead of staying in Vallejo. My mother had left us the house, which my sister decided to stay in, but I couldn't stay there without her. In LA I worked out with some professional basketball players. I was away from the crime and grime of Oakland and I was able to soak up a new life. At this time my agent, Top Allen, was looking for positions for me in the NBA. But with my mind set on nothing less than an NBA contract, I turned down some other opportunities. My friend Carlton was working as a loan officer, so I took a job with his company to keep funds flowing. To keep my basketball skills sharp, I played in the San Francisco Pro-Am League, as I had done every summer after high school.

The Pro-Am League begins when every other basketball league is finished, and players from all over California come to San Francisco to play for the summer. Each team is allowed three NBA players, two European players, four NCAA All-Americans, and three high school All-Americans. The league didn't pay, but it was a great opportunity to play with some incredible talent.

AND1 AND "AIR CANADA"

During my year working as a loan officer I was offered opportunities to play basketball in Europe, but fear of the unknown kept me from accepting. It was during this time that the AND1 Streetball Team had been touring through the US. They stopped in San Francisco to promote tryouts for local players who would form the team that would play against them. The ten best local players would be picked. At the end of the tour, the best player from each stop was promised a spot in the Hall of Fame game at the end of the tour, and the best player in this final game would receive a paid contract with AND1.

I made the team to play against the AND1 team in San Francisco, played the best on our team, and won my spot in the Hall of Fame game. I won the MVP of this game and signed my contract with AND1. This was a huge accomplishment for me, since the AND1 players were superstars in the basketball world. I toured with AND1, all over the United States, for three years. I got to live my life on the road with fans screaming everywhere we went. During the tour we filmed a reality show that was aired on national sports TV channels: AND1 Mixtape Tour. With the cameras following us we would often act up and not behave like ourselves, but by the end of the taping season the cameras would remain hidden in order to catch us as we really were.

The other members of the team kept comparing me to Vince Carter because of how high I could jump—at that time I had a 43-inch vertical. They started to call me "Air Canada the Jet," because I would soar and take people with me for a ride when I dunked. "Air Canada" would be my name from then on.

At this time my notoriety was sky high. If I walked down the street people would run up to me for autographs. I can remember being approached by Angela Bassett in Springfield, Massachusetts, where she asked for my autograph. I met Common, the singer and actor, at another game. Having these people come up to me and know my name was unbelievable. During my second year with AND1, singer Chris Brown toured a few dates with our team and travelled on our bus. We even got to play against a variety of guest celebrities, such as Lil Wayne and Fabolous to name a few. The games would be intense, the arenas packed full of high-energy fans. We never knew who might show up at some of our games—celebrities and NBA players would often stop in to catch some of the action. We had all come from the streets and were in our glory playing this type of basketball: no rules, no boundaries.

But the life of a touring basketball superstar in the streetball empire eventually became too much for me. The games were not as challenging as I wanted (we knew every game would be a winner for us and this became boring). It was not the life I believed I was destined for. I started to play less and less, focusing instead on my goal of playing professional basketball for a structured organization.

ITALY

A blessing came in the form of a phone call from my agent, who presented me with an opportunity to play overseas in Rome. I accepted and signed an eight-month contract. I stayed only a month. I began to feel homesick for the sunshine of California. I had the consistent feeling that I was missing something at home and wanted to return to what I knew best. I continued to worry about my sister. After protecting her my whole life, I felt as though I was abandoning her by leaving her behind in California. Subconsciously, I found I was comparing myself to my brother Terrill, when he had left us in 69th Village.

I did enjoy my time in Italy, however: I ate some of the best food I have ever tasted in my life. But I still found myself lonely. The romance of the city was meant for couples, and my mind was in a difference place. I knew I needed to go home. My faith told me that everything would be okay in the long run. When I returned my friends were disappointed in my lack of dedication. They wanted me to accomplish something with my basketball skills. I made excuses for having left, telling people I hadn't been treated properly and couldn't stand it any longer. But it was my mental and spiritual well-being that had been hurting.

When I got home, what I thought I had been missing was nothing at all. I was stuck at a dead end. My lack of focus and determination left me disappointed. I left

Italy with my signing bonus and first month's pay, and I spent my time back in California focusing on basketball and drumming. I practiced and worked out with a personal trainer, and played the drums at church and choir rehearsals.

A New Opportunity

The summer after I returned from Italy, I went back to the Pro-Am League, when I was first introduced to Andre Levingston, the owner of a brand new team in the American Basketball Association (ABA), the Halifax Rainmen. I remember that encounter like it was five minutes ago. He came to speak to me after a game because he wanted to see what I could offer the new team he was starting in Nova Scotia. Not having any idea where Halifax or Nova Scotia were, I immediately turned him down and laughed in his face. I had already been in contact with a team in Japan, so I was completely uninterested in what Andre had to say. I turned him down with arrogance and ignorance, and walked away with no intention of giving him or his team a chance.

After a month or so, the contract with Japan fell through. My agent phoned Andre in Halifax and asked if a deal was still on the table. Andre had been so unimpressed with my attitude during our first meeting that he swore he would never accept me as a member of his team. It seemed as though my opportunity with the Rainmen was out the window. But my talent spoke for me, and Andre eventually changed his mind. He offered me a position as starting forward for the Halifax Rainmen.

Off to Halifax

It was my grandmother who pushed me to sign a contract with the Rainmen. She knew that I needed to get away from California and the life I had been leading there after my mother's passing. The fear of leaving my sister alone while I was in Italy had brought me home, but the fact that I would actually need to go away to take care of her was the reality that brought me to Halifax.

I knew that I would need the clarity of a different life in order to be the supportive brother Shirley needed, spiritually and emotionally. My focus would now be solely on my craft.

October 15, 2007, was the day I first landed in Halifax. I remember the scent of the fresh, fall air. I was so used to the smell of pollution, and this air was so pure. I can remember being picked up at the airport, and taken for a tour of Halifax. The "bad" neighbourhoods here were like the upscale ones where I was from. I also remember trying to throw things in the garbage during my first few weeks, and feeling like I was taking a test every time. I seemed like I would stand there for longer than the flight from California had taken. It took me awhile, but I finally got used to the concepts of recycling and composting.

I was homesick during the first few weeks. It was a constant battle with myself to stay, when I wanted so badly to return home. But, surrounded by genuine Maritime hospitality, I soon knew that I would be able to make it. In California people tend to keep to themselves. I found that being in Halifax reminded me of the Southern hospitality in Texas. People in Halifax were ready to do anything for me, without expecting anything in return. People were all too anxious to feed me as soon as I walked into their home. It took me a while to adapt to this mentality. One lesson I had to learn was to take my shoes off at the front door. In the US, your shoes would stay on your feet in anyone's house. Not in Halifax. I noticed the genuine kindness in this city just days after arriving. I was a stranger, and yet I was accepted so easily.

Not long after I arrived I met Dawn Rudolph. Her company shared a space with the Rainmen office, and when the team began to feel homesick she went out and bought us all Christmas presents. Each player received a gift bag with an Edge razor. Being the only player who used this type of razor, I ended up with all fifteen and was thrilled. I had no idea the effect this woman would have on the rest of my life.

The city treated me like a king from the moment I arrived. From day one I was the focus of the organization, which only encouraged my ego, and I began to feel like I was untouchable again. I had come from a huge city with a lot of talented celebrity players, to this small city that appreciated my talent. After three days of getting to know my team, learning the city, and trying my first donair, training camp began. My teammates and I hopped on a bus to the small town of Bridgewater, where we practiced three times a day: 6:00–8:00 A.M., 1:00–2:30 P.M., and 6:00–8:00 P.M. This went on for two full weeks. We were isolated. The only accessible phones were in our hotel rooms, with no long distance. Training hard every single day, with only our teammates to lean on, made us form a bond that would prepare us for the tough season ahead. We were now a basketball family.

Halifax Royalty

After training camp we returned to Halifax. The owner and our coach gave us the week off to rest our bodies, but there was no rest for us. We found ourselves out on the town every night. The "Halifax Rainmen" name became known in the city before our season even began. We loved the attention. Just the rumour of my talent had brought me fame everywhere in Halifax. I wondered how I could ever go back to California and leave this spotlight I had created before I had even proven myself on the court. I couldn't see that all of this would eventually turn on me.

This lifestyle began to tarnish the name I had worked to create. I began to get a reputation, and I had to again learn the hard way that my ego would not take me through all of this untarnished. This game started to run my life and became too much to handle, and ultimately had a negative effect on my game on the court.

Tamara

Just after our first season of training camp, the team wanted to go out for a night on the town. The club we chose was packed and the lineup was down the street.

My mom, Yvonne Crookshank, my older brother Terrill at age three, and myself at age two months.

Shirley Crookshank, my grandmother and guardian angel.

(Above) A typical day in Texas: my father in his uniform (no shirt, no shoes), my mother coming to check on everyone, and us kids on the steps. I am at the bottom right.

(Right) My school picture at age eight. I was going home to count my father's money at this age.

Dominating the game and taking the streets to the court against Boo Jackson of the Quebec Kebs. -Scott Kirkpatrick, stkPhoto

Tip off against the Oshawa Power. -Scott Kirkpatrick, stkPhoto

"Air Canada" takes flight! -Scott Kirkpatrick, stkPhoto

Having my way with the London Lightning during the championship series. -Scott Kirkpatrick, stkPhoto

Dunking on Oshawa players. -Scott Kirkpatrick, stkPhoto

Standing proud with my family on the sidelines. -Scott Kirkpatrick, stkPhoto

Going hard in the paint against Oshawa. -Scott Kirkpatrick, stkPhoto

Engaging a fan after a speech in Tantallon, NS. -Scott Kirkpatrick, stkPhoto

My beautiful princess, Layla. She is my life. -Scott Kirkpatrick, stkPhoto

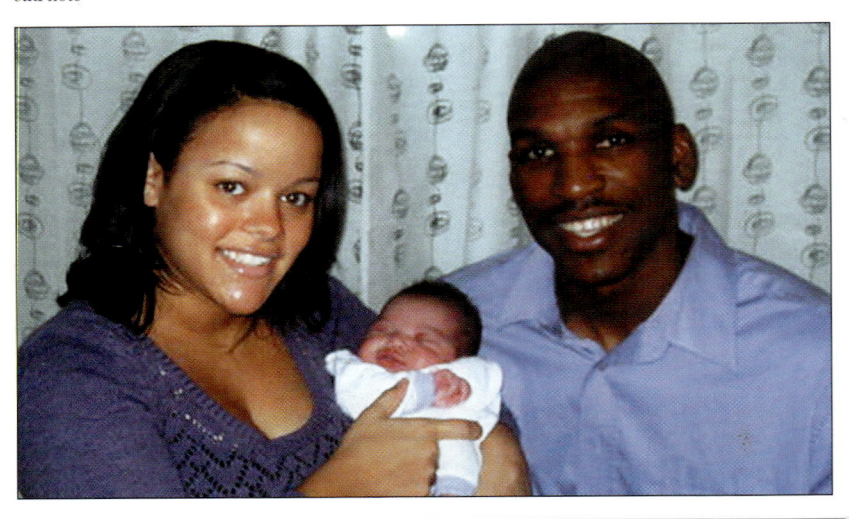

Tamara, Layla, and I.

The group of us tall Americans stuck out. I looked past the crowd of people and saw a woman standing alone towards the back of the room. I walked over to her and told her she was so tiny, joking that she was the size of a Cheerio. She told me her name was Tamara and the reason she didn't look like she was having a great time was because she had been dragged out for her friend's party and really didn't want to be there. I started to talk to the friend she was with and even dated her for a little while, but when that relationship died off I kept in contact with this tiny person I had quickly become very fond of.

Returning to Faith

In the summer of 2009, when I needed a place to stay, Tamara offered her extra bedroom. We had become close, like a brother and sister at this point. We spent a lot of time together, and when she began to see that I had a strong connection to my faith she asked me to go to church with her. At first, I told her that I had been scarred by church in my life and wasn't sure if I wanted to get involved again. I agreed to go with her from time to time, but I was still battling with the grudge I felt against my faith after my mother's passing.

Tamara would ask me every week if I wanted to go to church with her. I always had an excuse why I couldn't or wouldn't go. I went a few times during my second season, and one Sunday their drummer didn't show up for the service. I walked up to the drum set, sat down, and started to play—people watched with their eyes wide open. That drum set is still smoking! The release I felt after playing that Sunday surprised me. I didn't realize how much I had missed playing. The congregation was extremely supportive and encouraged me to continue drumming on Sundays. My craving to be on the drums meant that I began to attend church more and more. Soon my focus began to shift from the party life and toward my faith, drumming, and my new church family.

Being in church kept me in a better place. I found myself less angry, as if giving my faith another chance was healing the pain I had felt in my soul for so long. I saw that I had been in the wrong. Before, I had seen death as a punishment for something my family must have done. I now began to see that death was a part of life.

I was doing so well on the court, with sponsors, achievements, and personal goals, that my ego started to grow again. But being in church continued to humble me, bring me back down to reality, and show me that I did need my faith. I wanted to get more involved, so Tamara and I started going to Bible study classes every Tuesday. A group of about fifteen churchgoers, we got together to discuss faith. It became the place where we were able to release our stresses each week.

Jonathan Bell ran these Tuesday sessions, and he has since become my spiritual mentor. Throughout the day he sends me scriptures—he always seems to know what I need. I can rely on him for guidance and a supportive word at any time, in any situation. He holds me accountable for my actions, but gives me confidence when I am feeling down. In my weak moments, Jonathan asks the questions I need to hear, and I know that he will always guide me toward the positive things in life, and keep me from negative influences. With Jonathan and Tamara's help I started to rebuild a trust in my faith.

2007-08

In my first season with the Rainmen I averaged 22 points and 12 rebounds per game. Only a few games into the season, the owner approached me with an offer from Coca-Cola: they wanted to sponsor me. This meant I would be the first player in the ABL to receive a sponsorship deal. Coming from a boy in the projects to the man who would walk into grocery stores, pharmacies, and corner stores to see his billboard looking back at him was unreal. My face was everywhere that first season, and my family was so proud.

When the basketball season was finished I returned home to California for a month. The month I was home was my summer break, as I had signed to play in Finland, on the Componeta Karkkila second division team, for the remainder of the summer months. The time I spent in Finland was memorable, but not overly enjoyable. The last two weeks of my stay were spent in complete darkness. It was their leap year, when the sun would set for weeks at a time. Being from California—the land of sun and sand—the total darkness was hard to take. I was happy to land back in California, ready to train and negotiate for the next season.

2008-09

When I returned to Halifax for my second season with the Rainmen, I knew I needed to focus my mind on my career. However, I found myself arguing with the team's coach, questioning his judgement and his decisions. The whole team felt the same, but I became the voice of our concerns. After the second game of the regular season, the owner called me into his office to meet with him and the coach. He was extremely upset, but backed the coach's decision to put me on indefinite suspension for a full year, starting immediately.

My punishment was to go into local schools to speak to students about the consequences of our actions. The suspension was an over-the-top reaction to my behaviour, but with the coach also the general manager of the team and making all the decisions, I was unable to argue his ruling. My immediate reaction was to question my faith: how could I end up in this situation? With everything I had overcome in my life, I was still unable to complete the season in the sport that I loved.

With little explanation as to why I had been suspended, the media storm was incredible. Rumours circulated about me being involved in serious criminal activities. The week following the announcement of my suspension I had to stay in the Westin Hotel just to keep away from the media attention. This was an extremely hard time for me. The stress of the disappointment and the extent of the negative attention of all of this were difficult to handle. I was told not to speak with any media or my pay would be suspended as well. This made me feel isolated and unable to defend myself. My coach told me that my attitude was destructive. I couldn't understand this, and the confusion began to eat away at me. My friend Carlton flew from California overnight to make sure my mental health remained intact.

Halifax Comes to the Rescue

My talent on the court was needed to keep the team on the path to a championship. Fans began to email the team owner, and the media was bombarded with support for my return to the court. The loyalty of my fan base was humbling: people were demanding refunds on their season tickets, campaigning for my return, and defending my character all over the city. Since I was able to talk in elementary schools and was still on the team's payroll, people knew that the reasons behind my suspension could not have been as dramatic as the rumours suggested.

When I found out just how much the city had embraced me, I decided it was time to grow up. I didn't want to let my fans down, especially since they had gone to war for me in my time of need. During that period of about six weeks, it had actually become easier for me to stay in Halifax. All that time I had been speaking to young kids in local schools about adversity and overcoming obstacles. This meant I had no choice but to get over my feeling of homesickness. I would tell young people that others would judge them in life, but to not allow people to change who they were. Through the adversity of getting suspended, I had discovered another calling: public speaking. Any opportunity the team was given to speak in public from then on, I was the first to offer my services.

Return to the Court

My suspension was overturned after seven games. I received a phone call from the owner on February 6, 2009, telling me that I needed to be ready for some changes and should be getting back in the gym. The next morning, I woke up to headlines in the paper saying that the head coach and general manager of the Halifax Rainmen had been fired, and I was going to be returning to the court.

That Sunday I was back in action. I found myself realizing that the struggles I had gone through earlier in my life—including the drugs, violence, and the passing of my mother—had made this situation much easier to bear. I came onto the court, my first game back from suspension, to play the Vermont Frost Heaves. It was a Sunday afternoon, and there were only a few empty seats in the Metro Centre's lower bowl. When my name was called at the beginning of the game, the sound in the Metro Centre was overwhelming. These were my fans, and they came out in full force to support my return. I returned to the court harder and prouder than ever before. I had officially become a Haligonian.

My first game back was also Tony Bennett's first game with the team. I can remember him throwing me an alley-oop, which drove the crowd wild. I scored 21 points and had 18 rebounds that game. I can still taste the popcorn I snuck from a courtside fan. Just being back on the court made me feel free. The game went by so fast. I was back on stage, playing with my family: the guys that I had endured training camp with.

It was one of the most challenging games I've ever played. Our team had come up against the Frost Heaves three times while I had been suspended, and lost all three games. I knew that if I could help the team win this game, then I really would have made a difference. And I did. We won that game. Coach Les Barry had only just started his career with the Rainmen that game, and had already led us to beat the Vermont Frost Heaves for the first time that season. Playing that Sunday allowed me to forget about all the negativity I had been through during the prior weeks.

A Gift of Second Chances

When I first met Dawn Rudolph during my first season, I would go sit with her in our shared Rainmen office. I used to joke with her that she always seemed to have snacks. I still tease her about this. During my second year I would go to lunch with her. She would ask about my life and seemed to really care. I immediately felt a connection with her beautiful spirit. I knew I could trust her.

One day I needed her advice. While I was sitting in her office talking, I noticed a newspaper article on her wall about her being a breast cancer survivor. I was impressed that she had beaten cancer and was still this lively and beautiful person. The way I felt, listening to her describe beating cancer while my mother had just passed away from ovarian cancer, was indescribable. I remember feeling a stinging in my gut at the thought that cancer allowed some people to live, and took others away from their families. I opened my heart and shared my stories, and in return she embraced me. She asked if I would like to come for dinner to meet her family—her husband, Gary, and two children, Brooke and Michael. I was honoured and accepted. I instantly felt a connection with the whole family. This beautiful woman very quickly became a rock in my life. She has become my Canadian mother.

I could see that my struggles in life affected her greatly. During my suspension, I had to sit on the bench and watch the games without being able to touch the court. This was hard for me, but when a new player was brought in to play in my place, with my number 20 jersey, this really weighed on Dawn. She went up to the top of the section where she had held season tickets to Rainmen games since day one. She couldn't watch the game anymore, knowing that I was courtside and another player was playing with my number. She called me after the game and told me how much it bothered her to see me suffering. From that day on I knew that our relationship was real. That was when I started to call her mom.

Dawn would call to make sure I had eaten or to ask if I needed anything. She was always checking on me, and had something to say when I was eating a lot of fast food; a heavy sigh was the reaction I got to my unhealthy habits. Today she is my mother, in all aspects of the word, and I am always able to lean on her for support. She proudly calls me son, and gets quite defensive when someone jokingly suggests, "one of these things is not like the others." Her children call me their brother. Brooke, who is now sixteen, will explain our relationship by simply suggesting people watch the movie *The Blind Side*. Michael, now nineteen, was just accepted to Mount Allison University in New Brunswick, and is very much my little brother.

As our relationship grew, and I learned more about Dawn's survival and she learned more about mine, it seemed as though we had both been given a second chance: me with a mom, and her with life. Feeling that my life was becoming more and more positive, I was given the chance to prove myself by being a good son to her. To this day I find myself achieving great things to make her proud. She has added light into my soul again, and I can see my future only getting better. I knew she was an angel disguised as a second mom for me as she takes the most pride in two things: her family and her garden. I had become a part of her family, but when I was recruited to become part of her garden I knew there was no going back.

Layla

Meanwhile during this time Tamara and I began to rely more on each other. She would help me out at my summer camps at the registration table and I would go to her for advice and support. During the summer between my second and third seasons with the Rainmen she phoned me excited about a new job she had just accepted. I told her we would need to celebrate. After this we became inseparable, and our relationship developed from best friends into something even more meaningful.

Three weeks later I went home to California for a visit. I talked to Tamara every day. We knew that we needed to keep our relationship strong because we relied so heavily on each other's support. One day she phoned and seemed concerned about having been sick for the past few days, so she booked an appointment to see the doctor. When the results came back we found out she was pregnant with my child.

I returned to Halifax the next week to support Tamara. We both felt concerns about having a child at that point in our lives. We knew that it would be an adjustment. It took about a month for me to really come to terms with this reality. I then embraced the thought of having a child and devoted the next eight months to making every appointment and catering to everything she needed. I sat as moral support through months of morning sickness. I wanted to do everything I could to help her in any way. I thought we would be having a son, but others told me that people like me have daughters to slow them down.

At this point my life off the court was content, which made me play even better on the court. This is the year, 2010, that I was named MVP. I played every game except one in Puerto Rico that was scheduled the same day our baby was due. One week after that game, on February 16, 2010, at 11:55 P.M., we were blessed with a daughter, my beautiful Layla Elizabeth. She was nine pounds, eleven ounces, and twenty-one inches long. I cried when I saw my new baby girl. I prayed over her tiny body. I felt this was my opportunity to be a great father, to love my child as my mother had loved me. I wanted to show her how a father should love and nurture his child no matter what. The whole team was supportive throughout the process and were excited to see our brand new baby. I would bring week-old Layla to practice, not wanting to be away from her for any time at all. It was the best feeling in the world, to have made something so beautiful.

Once again, my perspective in life had changed. I went from counting thousands of dollars in Galveston, struggling to survive in Oakland, enduring a difficult death in Vallejo, starting a positive career in Halifax, to seeing my precious daughter, Layla. I had been through adversities in my life and now it was time to be an example to others of how to handle those adversities. I vowed to create a better life for my new daughter. It would be easier to stay focused with two parents that take pride in parenting and raising a child in a positive environment. Tamara and I have set schedules and routines for her, and teach her healthy living habits, discipline, and respect.

My life has changed drastically, knowing that if I take myself back down those hard roads that I came from, I would not only lose my life but my daughter would lose her father. My job is to pave a way for her so when she gets older she can have a great example of how to become something from nothing. I strive to be the best role model I can be.

Chapter 4
"Air Canada" Takes Off

Playing basketball was not a job for me but the great love of my life. Kids looked up to me for entertainment as well as for my talents. At the league's all-star game in Halifax in 2010, I came to the dunk contest dressed head to toe as Superman. The roar of laugher in the arena was energizing, and I won the contest. That stunt still makes my fans laugh.

The most difficult player I ever had to defend was Elvin Mims, who played for the Lawton-Fort Sill Calvary. I had so much respect for him. Facing him was like playing chess on the court: I would think I had figured out his strategy, but he would change his methods in an instant. But one of my favourite teams to play in the PBL and NBL was the Laval Kebs. Aaron Spears was the centre for their team, and he and I had an ongoing feud. I made it my mission to get inside his head every single game, and I knew how to push his buttons.

A lot of basketball players find defence difficult because it's extremely tiring. I get my mind away from being tired by thinking about my mother on her deathbed. I think to myself: *If she could still fight then, I am able to fight through this now.* So there's my secret: I am a great defensive player because the thought of my mother boosts my energy. I saw the offensive players I was guarding as victims of my talent. If they had a weakness I was going to expose it. I used to tell these opponents before games that there was no one else on the court but them and me. I would get inside their heads and frustrate them out of their game. I would challenge their thoughts on the court, and try to take them out of their comfort zones.

2010-11

On a basketball team, the coach is like your father. We had accepted our coach through training camp and had brought his ideas and his theories to the court. When our coach, Les Berry, left the team in January 2011, it uprooted the foundation of the team. Players would always come and go, which affects the team, but taking the father of the team away causes a whole different set of issues.

We would bounce back from this change, however: we added coach Mike Evans to our family. His spirit commanded the team's loyalty. He had a giving heart, and would truly pay attention to the needs of his team. He cared about our personal lives and created a team charisma that had previously been lacking. His strategies were different, but he held us all accountable. He allowed us to be men: we had no curfews, and there was no belittling us or controlling us off the court. He told us that if our off-the-court conduct affected our on-the-court performance there would be consequences, and he held us to that. He also created a freedom within the organization where we were able to express our feelings and discuss anything that was bothering us without any judgement. We all trusted him. That season he led us to the semi-finals against Lawton-Fort Sill, where we lost in game three of a three-game series. Our success that season showed us that if a coach committed to his team like a father committed to his family, then the team can accomplish a lot more.

New League and New Coach

During my fifth season I knew I needed to lend myself to the team for the greater good. I had been meeting my personal goals, but I wasn't helping my teammates' stats, so I made the decision to be more team-oriented. This year, everyone was loyal to the team—there was no one player out for himself—and I believe this is the reason we made it as far as we did.

The 2011–12 season is one that I will never forget. Once again, our coach changed. Coach Evans had opportunities elsewhere and did not renew his contract with the Rainmen. This left me in a sad state as I had really felt a connection and a loyalty to him. We were introduced to our new coach at the beginning of training camp in September of 2011. Our newest addition was Coach Pep Claros, and he was definitely unique. His coaching strategies were unlike anything any of us had been through before. But with his broken English and loud, expressive gestures, he led the Halifax Rainmen into a new era: our first season in the brand new National Basketball League of Canada (NBL).

Coach Pep's pre-game shouting—which he referred to as speeches—were always exciting and inspirational. He put his heart and soul into our team, which made us want to give ours as well. It wasn't above Coach Pep to yell, jump on tables, and argue calls that were probably accurate. Huddles with him were also entertaining. His excited "pep" talks sounded like Spanish to us, but we listened intently to the few words we could actually understand. Coach Pep inspired all of us to become more family oriented, as he had brought his wife and two children with him from Spain. This made it easier for me to be a father and a basketball player, and I played even better and harder than before.

By the end of my fifth season with the Rainmen I could feel the wear and tear my career was having on my body. I was starting to ache after every game. The only thing that kept me energetic and ready to go every night was the atmosphere the fans created. Every time I stepped onto the court, the fans would be on their feet screaming my name, with admiration in their eyes and support written all over their handmade signs. There is nothing like the feeling of support from three thousand plus fans. You know they're there to cheer you on, and they have just as much invested in the outcome of the game as you do. The smell of popcorn, the sound of loud music, the feeling of victory already in the air, all give me the urge to prove to the fans that I'm worthy of their screams.

We dominated a huge portion of the season, and went on a ten-game winning streak. Coach Pep made us feel untouchable, and we fought hard to make him proud. The only obstacle that stood in our way was the London Lightning, who had been the dominant team in the PBL as well. They were the roadblock to our team's success. We played London in the league championship series. In a five-game fight, it came down to the absolute end. With players injured and pride set aside, we fought with everything we had for our coach, for our fans, and for ourselves.

The NBL Playoffs

The playoffs began with us taking on the Laval Kebs in a three-game series. We beat them terribly in their own house in game one, then came home to lose game two and win game three—this put us into the finals, for the long-awaited chance to meet our rivals from London.

Getting to a championship series was something that I had strived for my whole career. I knew that as the years went on I would have less time to accomplish this goal, so attaining it in my fifth season was a blessing. The series was highly anticipated, and our away games were broadcast on Eastlink TV so that our fans at home could watch live while we played our hearts out. The response was unbelievable: we had more support than we ever expected. It seemed like the whole city was talking about us.

The rivalry between our two teams was intense, and our eagerness to pull off a win was overwhelming. London's star player and fan favourite, Gabe Freeman, had been my number one competition, as he and I had been competing against each other for years. Our styles were much the same, which made it easy for me to be hated in London just as he was hated in Halifax. Before the series started, we studied game tapes and I made sure I analyzed each move Gabe used in every game. We were on our way to a city that was wholeheartedly behind its team and we knew the atmosphere there would be hugely one-sided. Their stadium could get so loud that it would make it hard to think or hear. London had already declared game one a victory before we even stepped on the court.

On the plane to London the day before game one, you could see the tension in our team. Game rituals were thrown off, the quiet players were becoming the jokesters, and the loud players sat with their headphones snugly over their ears. When we arrived in London the sun was out, and so were the journalists, who waited for us as we got off the plane.

Games One and Two
March 18 and 19, 2012

I did not eat the whole day before game one. The pressure to make our fans proud was weighing on all of us. It would make winning the title worth so much more knowing that so many people were counting on us.

The day of game one I was up at 5:00 A.M. and couldn't sleep. I left my hotel room and went for a walk around the city to put myself at ease. At 9:00 A.M. I met the team in the lobby and we headed to the arena for a shootaround. As we walked in, I started to play the game out in my head. Five years with the Rainmen organization and everything I had been waiting for would happen that night. We went back to the hotel to rest and met for lunch. Many players didn't show up, too nervous to eat. The hours before the game felt like days. I decided my goal for the series was to be the best defender I could be.

As we walked back into the arena two hours before the game, fans were already lined up, taunting us as we walked in. I can remember the shouts of "Crookshank you suck!" This made me smile: I guess I was so bad that it made them all remember me. Soon, it was game time. The national anthem rang loudly through the stadium. I stood with my team focused on what I needed to accomplish that night, and anxious for the jump ball and the start of the game. Our only objective was to win. It is usually the home team that comes out strong, but as the road team we changed that trend and went hard at the London players.

The game started with us on the scoreboard first, and then it continued back and forth. We kept pace with them and played with everything we had. We knew we would have to tire them out, so Coach Pep made lots of substitutions. His strategy worked, as we had London exhausted by the third quarter. We went into the fourth quarter tied, leaving us the perfect opportunity to win game one. In the fourth quarter we defeated ourselves, paying more attention to the time left on the clock than to the task at hand. We lost that game by only three points. Afterwards, we looked forward instead of dwelling on the loss. We were all anxious to play game two the next day. With our collective confidence only slightly shaken, we returned to our hotel to rest, and prepare for battle again the next night.

Day two was a bit more difficult than the day before. We had to shake off the loss and prepare ourselves to push even harder. But game two was a runaway: London came out strong and kept their lead the whole game, winning easily. But we left that night knowing that the series was about to change. Going home to our own court and the support of our fans, we knew we were guaranteed to win the next two games.

Home Court Advantage: Games Three and Four
March 21 and 22, 2012

When we arrived back in Halifax the next day the whole city was on fire with excitement. The London players kept taunting us, saying the series was about to be a sweep. Even their coach, Micheal Ray Richardson, showed up to shootaround the morning of game three with a broom in tow. Lightly sweeping at the court, arrogance plastered across his face, his efforts to shake us were pointless. His little display just made us want the win even more.

Game three was do or die for us. If we lost game three, the series was over. Feeling the pressure, we came out with mistakes early in the game and quickly found ourselves up against a wall. We had started behind by 5 or 6 points, and then all off a sudden we were behind by 16. We knew we had to battle back from this, so we put our heads down and ran at it full speed. Helping us with that charge were our loyal fans. On their feet and screaming, they kept their faith in us and we wanted to show them we could win. We took advantage of every play, and chipped away at London's lead. Because I am known to bring a lot of energy to the team, I knew I would have to pump everyone up even more if we were going to win the game. While I was defending one of London's players, he got called for holding the ball too long, which was a turnover. I ran down the court beating my chest and the crowd went wild.

During the fourth quarter, my aggressive defensive play caused me to foul out of the game. The last foul made my heart sink. I walked back to the bench for good with six minutes still left on the clock. It was the longest walk I've ever taken. We were down 10 points and I could no longer lead my team. I sat at the end of the bench with my stomach in my throat, my frustration plain to see. But even through all the adversity I had overcome, I had never been known to quit, so I put my frustration aside and became the biggest cheerleader in the building. Still down by 8 with three minutes left, I tried not to feel the championship slipping away. I wondered how we could have let this happen. We were fighting in our house and were close to getting swept in three straight games. This just made my shouts louder as I cheered from the sidelines.

When Gabe Freeman of London managed to catch his own rebound and dunk it, putting London ahead by six points, the air went out of the building. With less than a minute left in the game, I could see people leaving the arena, giving up on us. But the next minute was something those fans would regret missing.

Our point guard, Chris Hagan, came down the court and passed the ball to Joey Haywood right in front of our bench. He dribbled around his defender, pulled up for a three-point shot and scored! The fans were deafening. London tried to pass the ball in, but Lawrence Wright stole the ball and was fouled, making one free throw. We were now down only two points.

But with less than thirty seconds left, London made a layup and went back ahead by four. Joey Haywood then scored a quick basket for us. When London tried to pass the ball in, Lawrence Wright stole it passed to a teammate who missed his shot. But Wright was there for the rebound and scored. Two huge plays for Lawrence Wright and the game was tied!

Just after Wright scored, London tried to pass the ball far down the court, but threw it out of bounds with ten seconds left. In the meantime, I had turned from a player into a fan on the sidelines. London called a time out. Coach Pep hopped onto the scorers' table, making the fans go even wilder, before calling us into a huddle. We came in tight to hear what he had to say, and his words will stay with me always: "This is what you've been waiting for. All I can do now is coach. It's on you to want it. You can give them this game or you can take the game you were supposed to take anyway." My teammates went back onto the court full steam and set up a perfect screen, and Chris Hagan pulled up and made a perfect shot for the winning two points. The Metro Centre went completely crazy. The game was over and we had won. Following Coach Pep's lead, I jumped on the scorers' table and screamed with victory. It was an incredible feeling. The win gave us another opportunity to try to win the series. But we had to quickly clear our minds of that night's win, as game four was the next night, and we knew it would be just as much of a challenge.

The following night we were ready, and our confidence was unshakable. We kept the lead the whole game and won. There would be a game five with the winner of that game taking the championship.

Game Five
March 25, 2012

We travelled back to London for game five. We knew it was going to be hard to take the championship on London's home court, but we were ready for anything. When we arrived, we were ambushed by journalists and taunting fans all over the city. This only fuelled us on our mission. The atmosphere in the building before the game was incredible: the noise, the screams, the excitement. Playing in a big game like this had been my goal my whole career and I had finally arrived. I got a chance to talk to my team before the game. I told them no matter the outcome of the game, we were champions. I told them to never hang their heads, just to leave it all on the court and come out of this with nothing but pride.

As we walked onto the court the Jumbotron was showing a picture of Gabe Freeman and I, head-to-head, from game two. (That photo had been everywhere since that night, taken during a hostile moment of the game when Gabe and I had let our emotions get out of hand.) The game began and it was hard to hear anything on the court. We couldn't hear the plays being called, so we came up with a system of hand signals to communicate with each other. The game resembled the first game, with the tension and the energy in both teams. London wanted to show us that we shouldn't have won games two and three, while we wanted to show them that we could win the championship on their home court.

You would have thought we were playing Ping-Pong, the way the lead fluctuated back and forth. We found ourselves down by eight at halftime, but came back and made a run in the third quarter to tie the game. Going into the fourth quarter, London was up by four. Then the team's fans got involved in the game, and London walked all over us in the fourth quarter. The final score was 116-92 for London.

After the game the expressions on our team's faces were of pure devastation, a mixture of tears and anger. I couldn't help feeling disappointed, but I also felt extremely proud of my team and of myself. It was a hard fight, and even though we hadn't won the championship, we had battled our way to the very last quarter.

Chapter 5
Giving Back

For five years I was either captain or co-captain of the Rainmen. These were demanding roles to play because I had to be an example for the other players. I had to be on time, be consistent on the court, and honour all the team rules. I also needed to be a solid part of the community and remain professional on and off the court. I was a tour guide, guardian, support system, and family to my teammates.

Having grown up in California and witnessed countless celebrities never taking the time to inspire others, I knew I wanted to get involved in my community to do just that. I wanted to be an inspiration to children, especially to those who had very little at home. For two years I was involved in the Rainmen basketball camps, which gave me the chance to meet some of the children who attended our games. These were some of the fans who had been supporting me all season, and normally I wouldn't have had the opportunity to meet them.

I wanted to meet these kids to find out about their lives. They would tell me their favourite basketball players and what they wanted to do when they grew up. Seeing the looks on these kids' faces when they met me made me want to do more for them. They fed my soul with their dedication, and made me devote more to my training so that I could live up to their expectations of me. This became my definition of a role model: allowing them to inspire me.

I received the award for Rainman of the Year by *Faces* in 2010-2011, an honour given to the player who is most supported by the fans and most involved in the community. I was also named one of the top ten most famous people in Halifax by *Metro* in September 2010, next to some elite names like Ellen Page and Sidney Crosby. Everywhere I went people wanted to shake my hand

and talk about my game. Even today, I always stop and talk to my fans, and when I see kids playing basketball on street courts I try to stop and spend some time with them. I like to put smiles on these kids' faces because you never know what they might be going through. I remember driving down Lady Hammond Road in Halifax and seeing four children playing basketball on a street court. I passed by and thought: *if these kids are playing basketball, maybe they know me.* I pulled over, and when I got out they were shocked to see me. They asked me to show them some dunks and shoot around for a while. By the time I left, the kids looked thrilled.

I could see the effect I was having on the kids in the city when I was walking through the Halifax Shopping Centre and I approached a group of kids that had been following me. Their jaws dropped and one of them said: "You're Eric Crookshank!" I laughed and shook the kid's hand. I saw him later and he was still walking, in awe, clutching the hand I had shaken. I felt like Michael Jordan.

I was shocked to see that when a camp was set up with my name in Newfoundland there were eighty kids in attendance. I knew I had made a name for myself here in Halifax, but I had clearly established a fan base throughout the Atlantic provinces as well. I helped lead a four-day camp at Memorial University in St. John's, Newfoundland, with the local coach, past Rainmen player Peter Benoite, in the summer of 2010. I taught the group of ten- to twelve-year-olds in attendance some basic techniques on the court, and spoke to them about adversities they would encounter in their lives. I was also able to spend some time with the Memorial University players. They were excited by my presence and had lots of questions about my life.

CAM

During my first year in Halifax I met a boy named Cam. I asked him to hold my water bottle during a pre-season game at Saint Mary's University, so that my water wouldn't get taken by one of the other players. I threw the bottle to him, and he held it throughout the entire game, throwing it back to me at every break. I would have never thought that a water bottle would create such a connection.

I spoke to Cam and his parents after the game and they told me that he had autism. I soon became a permanent fixture in Cam's life. I began to mentor him, and tried my best to be a good role model. Cam and I developed a real bond, and he still phones me almost every week. And his parents still call when he gets himself in trouble, and he will listen to me. He refers to me as his big brother. I have a love for him that could never be replaced, because he has a determination that I admire.

John Strickland, "Strick"

I truly believe everything happens for a reason. The year I was suspended, the Rainmen wound up signing John Strickland, the streetball legend. Known as "Strick" to those around him, he taught me a lot. The fans loved him and embraced him instantly. Strick taught me how to involve my fans and make my show on the court more exciting. Every time I would make a show of something during a game, he would tell me what else I could do to make it that much better. He had a contagious spirit. You couldn't help but love him and laugh with him.

Early in the morning of October 6, 2010, the owner of the Rainmen called my cellphone. I knew it had to be something serious. He said that no one else knew but Strick's family, but since we had been such close friends, he wanted me to know before the news hit the media. Strick had died suddenly of a heart attack. The shock of his death took its toll on me. Only days before I had talked to him about his new position as general manager with the Rainmen. I had been negotiating with the Rainmen that summer and was still unsure if this was the place for me to stay. Strick wanted me to stay in Halifax with him, but if I wasn't going to play with the Rainmen he suggested he might have an opportunity for me to play with the Harlem Globetrotters. I was in New York in June 2010 when Strick called to invite me to show my talents to a few Globetrotter scouts that were in the city. I met Strick, with his permanent crooked grin in the lobby, for a pep talk before I got on the court. His mannerisms were uniquely his. His pep talk consisted of his usual drawn out "Come on Crooky." There was no hiding who he was. Strick was himself at all times, and his expectation was that everyone loved him, whether he was on the court or off. Everything seemed funnier when you were with him.

I had sent Strick a text message shortly before he died. I knew something must have been out of order because Strick always replied to me right away. Before his death, I had made a promise to myself not to get close to any players if I decided to stay with the Rainmen. I knew that players came and went, could be traded or released. I wanted to try to keep my emotions to myself so that it would affect me less when players left. After Strick was gone, it made me open my heart again: How could I not give these players the opportunity to change my life as Strick had?

Devon Norris

In the summer of 2009 I first met Devon Norris. As soon as we met I knew we would be great friends. He wanted to play with the Halifax Rainmen, so he would train with me every day in the hope of solidifying a position on the team for the next season. He has become one of my best friends in Halifax, and the two of us have organized children's camps that inspire younger children to follow their dreams, for the past two summers. Devon is the brain and the organizer behind our operation. He is a class act, and has determination on the court that I have seen in very few other people. He is a Dalhousie alumnus and is currently the assistant coach of their varsity basketball team.

TBear

A few years ago I met a local basketball star named Christian "TBear" Upshaw. He really stood out to me when I would go to see university games in the city. We knew each other and would occasionally speak, but we never really connected until last year. We would play together at open gyms and leagues in Halifax during the summer, and developed a real connection.

This past season, TBear tried out for the Halifax Rainmen and we became professional teammates. We would be roommates on the road, fighting like we grew up together: always bickering back and forth. TBear really embraced life as a member of the Halifax Rainmen. (He even wrote a song dedicated to his life with the team.) He has always been very well known in the local university basketball world and is loved and supported by his fans. I took TBear under my wing over the season and taught him how to play at the professional level. But more importantly, I taught him the value of being involved in the community and getting to know your supporters. We both really enjoy spending time with and mentoring children who have grown up in more difficult circumstances, and have became more like brothers than just friends. TBear now plays for the Moncton Miracles.

BCANS

Recently I was asked to be a guest speaker for the Pink Spring Celebration, a benefit supporting breast cancer research put on by Breast Cancer Action Nova Scotia (BCANS). I attended the benefit with my mom, and sister, Brooke, as my dates. I was given thirty minutes to speak to the crowd before I was auctioned off as a prize. (The winner would receive two hours of gym training with me).

I was honoured to have the opportunity to speak. But playing in front of thousands on the basketball court had never given me nerves like this. Speaking in front of survivors of cancer and newly diagnosed cancer patients, I knew I would have to get my mind in a different place. I didn't prepare a speech because I felt as though it had already been written. I was flattered that these women believed my words would affect people's lives, and that I would be able to make a difference with the stories of my own life and motivate people to continue to fight their battles.

Ola Brazil

My grandmother, Ola Brazil, was my father's mother and the leader of our family in so many ways. She is the one who led me to church, Compton Memorial Baptist Church in Galveston, for the first time. I used to dread going to church on Sundays. The only thing that kept my attention was watching the drummer. My grandmother was the one who encouraged me to pursue my interest in drumming.

Ola was a nurse at the University of Texas Medical Branch Hospital while I was growing up in Texas. She used to work the night shift—11:00 P.M. to 7:00 A.M.—but she would make sure we were in bed before she left. With my father preoccupied with his business in the streets, he wasn't usually home. My grandmother was very aware of the negative business my family members were involved in but she wouldn't scold or lecture them, she would simply pray for them.

One day, when it was forty-three degrees outside, I was in the car with her. I started teasing her and irritating her, and she sent me out of the car. I remember standing there in the heat for fifteen or twenty minutes before I knocked on the window and apologized, desperately needing air conditioning. The whole family respected and feared my grandmother.

I talked to my grandmother every single holiday, making sure she always knew how much I loved her. She didn't believe in cellphones so I would have to catch her at home. She would say, "If I wanted to talk to you, I would have asked you to come with me." Every time I went to visit Galveston I made sure that my grandmother was my first stop. I always made a point of spending some quality time with her.

I got a phone call from my cousin this year when everything was going really well with the basketball season. She told me that my grandmother had had a stroke, but that she was going to be okay. I had my doubts. I knew that my grandmother was getting older and that her body wasn't as strong as it had once been. Luckily I had been at practice when I got the call, and the team was there to support me through it. The stroke had left my grandmother unable to speak or to move her body, but because she was able to recognize her family, everyone felt like things were looking up.

A few days later, she stopped responding and slipped into a coma. The doctors thought that this was the end. The family made the decision to take her off life-support, and waited for her to quietly slip away in her sleep. The next morning, when the doctor went into her room, she was wide awake. She was sitting up, alert, and responsive. The rest of the family all had a chance to visit her in the hospital, and I was able to phone and speak to her. I could tell she was happy to hear from me, which warmed my heart. I received the final phone call the next day. She had passed away. I believe this was my grandmother's way of making sure she said goodbye to all the people who loved her so much.

I know that my grandmother had a great life. She had such a passion for everything she did. She will always be an influence in my life, and I celebrate all the lessons she taught me. She loved her family hard, worked hard, and played hard. I learned this from her: I play hard on the court and on the drums, I love hard, and I work hard. In remembrance of my grandmother I want to pass on all her great qualities to my children. I dedicate my hard work to her life. She led me to the drums, and every time I play them I play for her.

Passing on Lessons

Throughout the events in my life I have learned what I think are the most valuable lessons to teach to my children. I want them to know that respect is critical: respect for yourself, respect for your parents, and respect for others. You need to value and have respect for yourself before anyone can have respect for you. You need to have respect for your parents and their lessons in life because they have come before you and know what to expect. Respecting others and valuing their opinions will make them value and respect you in turn. I want to teach my children what my mother taught me: never to give up and that if you can dream of something then you can reach that dream. I will support my children in anything they want out of life as long as it is positive, and I want them to have unconditional faith in their religion. I have always been able to rely on my prayers and I want this for my children. I want to prevent my children from having to endure the struggles that I faced in my life, and I will work hard be a positive role model. When I look into my daughter's eyes I know that she deserves more than what I was given, and I want nothing more than to provide this for her.

Epilogue

Standing in St. Patrick's-Alexandra School with 160 eyes fixated on me, with children waiting to hear the next words out of my mouth, I think to myself: *When I was that age, I was watching people's lives stolen by gunshots and drugs in the 69th village of Oakland, California, and here they are looking to me as inspiration. Who am I today to motivate this type of admiration?*

I know now that when I talk to children I lead with my heart. I share my experiences in life to inspire them to live their lives in a positive way. I can see now that the events of my life have led me to where I am now, and that everything I've experienced has contributed its own worth to the man I am today. I can stand tall and embrace what I have become.

I want my message to be heard and understood: I want people to see that being a good person should be a goal in life, not an obligation. Judgement in life gets us nowhere, so we should concern ourselves with our own convictions and support the people we love through theirs. I aim not to push my belief system on anyone, but to show them how I managed my way through the obstacles I was dealt in life. My saviour has been my faith. I believe that having someone or something above you to believe in will help you through the hardest times in life.

Dreams are attainable, life is enjoyable, and love is what should always stay in your heart. Go away with the message that all obstacles can be overcome, and that the courage to handle the things you cannot control will come. Persevere through life and aim higher than you think you may be able. Keep in mind that if your dreams seem too high for you to grasp, I am 6'8" and always willing to reach with you.

ABOUT THE AUTHOR

Eric Crookshank began playing basketball in high school and has since played the game in a variety of different leagues, including the San Francisco Pro-Am League, NCAA, ABA, PBL, and National Basketball League of Canada as a member of the Halifax Rainmen, where he was the team's captain from 2007–2012. Now retired from the game he loves, he lives in Nova Scotia with his wife, Tamara, and daughter, Layla.